experience and a passion

**Rely on Thomas Cook as your
travelling companion on your next trip
and benefit from our unique heritage.**

Thomas Cook **pocket** guides

CANTERBURY

Thomas
Cook

Your travelling companion since 1873

Written by Debbie Stowe

Published by Thomas Cook Publishing
A division of Thomas Cook Tour Operations Limited
Company registration no. 3772199 England
The Thomas Cook Business Park, Unit 9, Coningsby Road,
Peterborough PE3 8SB, United Kingdom
Email: books@thomascook.com, Tel: +44 (0) 1733 416477
www.thomascookpublishing.com

Produced by Cambridge Publishing Management Limited
Burr Elm Court, Main Street, Caldecote CB23 7NU
www.cambridgepm.co.uk

ISBN: 978-1-84848-497-9

This first edition © 2011 Thomas Cook Publishing
Text © Thomas Cook Publishing
Cartography supplied by Redmoor Design, Tavistock, Devon
Map data © OpenStreetMap contributors CC-BY-SA, www.openstreetmap.org,
www.creativecommons.org

Series Editor: Karen Beaulah
Production/DTP: Steven Collins

Printed and bound in Spain by GraphyCems

Cover photography © Russell Kord/Alamy

CONTENTS

SYMBOLS KEY

The following symbols are used throughout this book:

ⓐ address 🕿 telephone ⓦ website address ⓔ email
🕒 opening times 🚇 public transport connections ❶ important

The following symbols are used on the maps:

🛈 information office		▪ point of interest
✈ airport		O city
🛡 police station		O large town
🚍 bus station		○ small town
🚆 railway station		═ motorway
✝ cathedral		— main road
✉ post office		minor road
❶ numbers denote featured		— railway
cafés, restaurants & venues		🅿🚌 park & ride

PRICE CATEGORIES

The ratings below indicate average price rates for a double room per night, including breakfast:

£ under £70 ££ £70–100 £££ over £100

The typical cost for a three-course meal without drinks, is as follows:

£ under £15 ££ £15–25 £££ over £25

🔾 *Christ Church Gate forms the entrance to the cathedral precinct*

INTRODUCING
Canterbury

Introduction

For a small town of around 40,000 people to be one of the most visited places in England suggests that there is something rather special about the place. And Canterbury does not disappoint. It has made an indelible imprint on the country's literary and religious life, and played a significant role in its history. The architectural inheritance of this distinguished history is an illustrious trio of holy buildings, St Martin's Church, St Augustine's Abbey and presided over by the glorious Canterbury Cathedral.

But a visit to this Kentish town does not only involve traipsing around worthy relics. It means a lot of fun. Chaucer's *The Canterbury Tales*, bane of GCSE English students up and down the land, has been reinvented as a hilariously kitsch attraction, rendering Old English tales as joyfully bawdy tableaux. And likewise, the museums detailing the town's history do so in a hands-on, engaging way.

The city's literary pedigree ensures that arts appetites will be more than sated, with two major theatres, including the brand spanking New Marlowe (named after Elizabethan dramatist Christopher, another Canterbury son), turning out culture from comedy to the classics. There is a wealth of charming venues in which to tend to culinary appetites, from olde-worlde tea rooms via medieval inns to top-notch restaurants.

There's also much enjoyment to be had in the open air. Merely meandering the cobbled streets at leisure, taking in the crooked Tudor houses and narrow lanes, is wonderfully rewarding. Two green spaces within the old city walls lend the place a pastoral air. The traditional British coastal resorts of Herne Bay and Whitstable are both at hand if you fancy being beside the seaside.

But it's another body of water that provides one of Canterbury's iconic pastimes: a punt along the River Stour. As you leisurely cruise down the gentle tributary, alongside and under the town's points of interest, regaled by your punter with fascinating anecdotes about the city, it is hard to imagine a better microcosm of all that is good about Canterbury. It's clear why the centuries have seen so many pilgrims, whether for piety or pleasure, flock to this extraordinary place.

🔺 *Canterbury Cathedral is – and has always been – a tourist magnet*

When to go

SEASONS & CLIMATE

Canterbury's many facets ensure that, whatever the time of the year or the weather, visitors will be pounding its cobbled streets. A-list attractions such as Canterbury Cathedral exert a pull that trumps the vicissitudes of the British climate. The compact centre of town means there are no long treks between one highlight and the next, so even in bad weather your exposure to the elements will be limited.

That said, there are more and less clement times of year to schedule your trip. Its position in Kent, in the southeast of England, protects Canterbury from the worst excesses of the English weather. Ideally, avoid the bleak midwinter (December to February), when temperature lows may be in the region of freezing and rain is more likely. Spring, summer and autumn all see showers, unexpected chills and climatic fluctuations. Equally, they can bring delightful bright and sunny spells. May or October may turn out warmer than August. Average summer highs are around 20°C, while winter lows plunge to about 2°C. Whenever you visit, come prepared with suitable clothing for every weather-related eventuality.

As mentioned, there is no tourist-free time in Canterbury, but school holidays and the October festival ramp up visitor levels even further, so bear this in mind with regards to accommodation.

ANNUAL EVENTS

Canterbury's calendar of events brims all year round, albeit with a shift to indoor happenings as the weather gets colder. The main event is the **Canterbury Festival** ( www.canterbury festival.co.uk), a fortnight of music, art, comedy and theatre in October. Billed as Kent's International Arts Festival, it is the largest event of its kind in the region and boasts an illustrious roster of past guests including T S Eliot and Dorothy Sayers. The rest of the calendar – which runs the gamut from half-marathons via walks, food festivals and cultural jamborees to the English eccentricity of hop hoodening (it involves a wooden horse) – is too extensive to detail here, but the town's official site has an exhaustive list, including descriptions, dates, times, locations and contact numbers. ⓦ www.canterbury.co.uk/events

All that remains of St George's Church after a World War II air raid

History

Inhabited since prehistoric times, Canterbury was captured in AD 43 by the Romans, who sent the occupying Celtic tribe packing. Their overthrow endowed the town with the typically Roman accoutrements – street grid system, theatre, forum, baths and the like – and a wall to keep out belligerent barbarians. After the Romans shipped out in AD 410 the place fell into disrepair, before Anglo-Saxons and Jutes from Denmark showed up, giving the town the name Cantwaraburh, or 'Kent people's stronghold'.

Meanwhile, over in Rome, fair-skinned children at a slave market had caught the eye of the future Pope Gregory. Told they were Angles (to which he punningly replied 'nay, but angels'), he subsequently dispatched a reluctant monk, Augustine, to

◆ *The city walls date back to William the Conqueror's time*

convert King Æthelberht of Kent to Christianity. Job done, Augustine made Canterbury a bishop's seat, precipitating much of the religious building work that defines the city today, and he became the first Archbishop of Canterbury. Buoyed by its new status, trade sprung up, cementing the town's reputation.

But its success was a double-edged sword. Several Danish attacks in the 9th and 10th centuries devastated Canterbury, and ensured that when William the Conqueror came marauding into town in 1066, the people did not resist. Just over a century later came one of the city's most notorious episodes, the murder of Archbishop Thomas Becket (see page 46) in the cathedral. This kick-started the pilgrimages subsequently immortalised by Chaucer in his seminal story collection *The Canterbury Tales*.

The Middle Ages heralded woe upon woe for Canterbury – the Black Death, general decline, the Peasants' Revolt, the Dissolution of the Monasteries, destruction or appropriation of various treasures, riots, revolt and finally surrender in the English Civil War (1642–51). But in 1830, what is said to be the world's first passenger railway opened between Canterbury and Whitstable and the city's population began to grow. Further pain was in store, though, during World War II when the Baedecker Blitz, the Nazis' bid to destroy the British attractions covered in the travel guide of the same name, targeted the town in 1942.

Post-war rebuilding endowed Canterbury with its university (Kent), and other cultural and retail developments followed. Its enduring importance has been recognised with visits from Pope John Paul II, the Queen and Mahatma Gandhi – not bad for such a small place.

Culture

With a heritage that is possibly unsurpassed in the United Kingdom outside London – quite remarkable for a town of such modest dimensions – Canterbury punches well above its weight, culturally speaking. The city is pivotal in two major works of English literature – Chaucer's magnum opus *The Canterbury Tales* and T S Eliot's haunting *Murder in the Cathedral* – and its traditions are showcased in an array of attractions and architectural landmarks. Museums deal with various facets of Canterbury's history, from the Romans to Bagpuss. Simply strolling the narrow streets, with their cobbles and beamed Tudor houses, is a cultural experience in itself.

The city also has a thriving contemporary cultural scene, boosted by the presence of the University of Kent. Many venues host musical happenings from big-name concerts to intimate gigs by lesser-known local performers. The polyphonic religious music of yore has gradually come to share the stage with the Canterbury Scene, a progressive rock, avant-garde and jazz movement that began in the 1960s. And the two-week Canterbury Festival in October is one of the top events in this part of the country.

◗ *Tower House stands in the lush West Gate Gardens (see pages 73–4)*

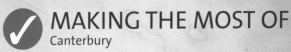

MAKING THE MOST OF
Canterbury

Shopping

Retailers have made the most of the throngs of visitors that flow through Canterbury, and the town has become something of a shopping destination – not least among continental Europeans when the Euro–Sterling exchange rate is favourable to them, particularly in the run-up to Christmas. But whether your business with the city's shops is about serious acquisitions or you're just browsing, shopping in Canterbury is a pleasant pastime.

The chief joy here is derived from the many tempting boutiques and independent shops. Most local businesses give a nod to their olde-worlde environs – even the local Starbucks looks traditional – creating an environment suited to the niche operator. Such outlets sell everything from delicious high-end comestibles like fudge and posh chocolates to books, antiques and fair-trade goods. The **King's Mile** (see page 51) is teeming with this type of place, and you can also try the quarters around **St Dunstan's Street**, **West Gate Towers** and **Northgate**.

Whitefriars Centre, the flagship multimillion-pound shopping centre, features the usual retail suspects including a **Fenwick** department store, which has become something of a Canterbury landmark and useful meeting and orientation point. It's an attractive retail development, consisting of open-air sections and the covered **Marlowe Arcade**, which has light flooding through a high ceiling, providing a pleasant atmosphere for shoppers. More mainstream retail branches can be found on and around the High Street, which is also home to a market on Wednesday and Friday.

For a memento of your trip, several of the main attractions, notably **Canterbury Cathedral**, the **Museum of Canterbury** and **The Canterbury Tales**, have well-stocked shops where you can pick up locally themed merchandise. Apt souvenirs include a copy of Chaucer's masterpiece *The Canterbury Tales*, if you've been inspired by your visit to Canterbury, or one of the many religious buys – from icons and choral CDs to 'cathedral ale'.

⬤ *The centre teems with quaint local shops and pubs*

Eating & drinking

Café culture is a real highlight of a Canterbury break. Quarters like Castle Street, Sun Street, Palace Street and the central thoroughfare – St Peter's Street, the High Street and St George's Street as you go from west to east – are full of tempting little places to stop for tea, coffee or a light lunch. Afternoon tea is an especially appealing English tradition, and so civilised!

Another type of eatery that you might fancy is the historic pub or inn, where hearty meals can be enjoyed as they have been by weary travellers over the last five centuries. If pub grub does not appeal (though much of it is high-end since the UK's gastro-pub revolution), simply enjoy a pint of beer or glass of wine.

If the weather's nice, there are several spots to enjoy lunch alfresco. **Solly's Orchard** near St Peter's Lane, **Dane John Gardens**, the **Franciscan Garden** and **West Gate Gardens** all provide fitting environs for eating – pop into one of the city's gourmet delis or the **Farmers' Market** near Canterbury West Railway Station to pick up provisions for a tasty picnic.

At the other end of the formality and expenditure scale, the city is home to several exclusive restaurants, and there's the odd Michelin star knocking around that will delight the deep-pocketed foodie.

Cafés are generally open from around 09.00 to 17.30 or 18.00. Some restaurants do a lunch shift from 12.00 to 14.30 or 15.00, then close until around 18.00; others stay open for the duration. With a few exceptions, most eateries close around 22.00, and your choice will decrease rapidly after then.

Canterbury cuisine is lacking a flagship dish but enticing UK staples such as a full English (calorific, fried) breakfast, Sunday roast and ploughman's lunch are all available. And the celebrated status of Kentish hops gives a historical slant to a pint of local beer.

⬤ *In a city full of pubs, you'll easily find one to suit your taste*

Entertainment

Gentility prevails in Canterbury, and its streets are happily free of the drunken hordes that blight many British cities. This is not to say that the fun ends when the sun goes down – quite the reverse. However, the more raucous revelry tends to take place in clubs on the outskirts of town. Central happenings are more sedate, such as the buskers who strum and sing on Burgate, right outside the entrance to the cathedral.

The large student body guarantees that there is plenty to whet the cultural appetite. Kent University organises a varied programme of events, and has a reputation for hosting big-ticket concerts (Led Zeppelin and The Cure are among the top performers to have rocked the city over the years). But the institution is just one of a series of venues in and around Canterbury that stage drama, music, dance and comedy. As you would expect from a town with the cultural kudos of Canterbury, the more highbrow disciplines, such as opera and ballet, are well represented. And film buffs of all proclivities – from mainstream popcorn movies to more arty visual fare – will find cinemas that cater to their needs.

To find out what's on during your stay, consult the official city website (Ⓦ www.canterbury.co.uk/events), which publishes a full calendar. The Visitor Centre (see page 93) should also be able to furnish you with information about upcoming events; the New Marlowe Theatre has a ticket desk here and the office staff can book tickets for several venues in Canterbury and outside. Larger venues typically sell tickets online or you may be able to buy them from an on-site box office.

If organised entertainment is a big draw for you, try to time your visit for October, when a smorgasbord of events is staged under the auspices of the fortnight-long Canterbury Festival.

◔ *The Canterbury Tales attraction tells Chaucer's story – the modern way*

Sport & relaxation

Golf

Putters and swingers have several options, including the 18-hole course at the 85-year-old Canterbury Golf Club and another at Broome Park.

Canterbury Golf Club ⓐ Scotland Hills, Littlebourne Road ⓣ 01227 453532 ⓦ www.canterburygolfclub.co.uk
Broome Park ⓐ Canterbury Road, Barham ⓣ 01227 830728 ⓦ www.broomepark.co.uk

Punting

One of the delights of a trip to Canterbury is a punt along the River Stour. Taking to the placid waters in a flat-bottomed boat, you glide tranquilly along while your punter (engine and guide in one) relates entertaining Canterbury anecdotes and describes the places you pass by – and under. An evening 'haunted river tour' is an alternative to the more serene daytime version. Particularly recommended is the **Canterbury Punting Company**; punts set off from the appropriately named Water Lane. Two rival firms also ply the waters.

Canterbury Punting Company ⓦ www.canterburypunting.co.uk
Canterbury River Navigation Company ⓦ www.crnc.co.uk
Canterbury Historic River Tours ⓦ www.canterburyrivertours.co.uk

Spas

Another way to relax is at the healing hands of a masseur, and there are plenty of spas in and around the city where you can have your stress pummelled into submission. The **Tor Spa**

Retreat in the village of Ickham, 8 km (5 miles) from Canterbury, is one of the plushest. ⓦ www.torsparetreat.com ⏱ 09.30–16.30 Tues & Thur–Sun, 14.00–21.00 Wed, closed Mon

Watersports
Out of town, Whitstable and Herne Bay both afford opportunities to get wet and wild in the English Channel, with kayaking, sailing, diving and waterskiing.

Spectator sports
Canterbury has a rugby and a football team and hosts many of Kent's cricket matches if you're in the mood for spectator sports.
Canterbury Rugby Football Club ⓦ www.cantrugby.co.uk
Canterbury City Football Club ⓦ www.canterburycityfc.org
Kent County Cricket Club ⓦ www.kentccc.com

⬤ *Nothing beats punting down the river on a sunny day*

Accommodation

As one of England's most visited cities, there is no shortage of places for modern-day pilgrims to rest their weary heads. The downside is that, because Canterbury is such a popular tourist destination, accommodation can be quite pricey. If your holiday budget is generous, it's possible to – sort of – follow in the footsteps of Chaucer's fictional creations and book into one of the historical hostelries in the centre of the city, some of which have been in operation for several centuries.

Encircling the city walls is a belt of bed and breakfast hotels (B&Bs), which offer more affordable rooms, some en-suite and others with shared wash facilities. If you have a car, you could probably shave another £10 or more off the price of a B&B by basing yourself outside Canterbury. Herne Bay, for example, is about a 20-minute drive. But this is really only worth doing if money is tight; if you're reliant on public transport the extra hassle and fares probably cancel out the cash gain. If you want to go rural, rent a cottage in the verdant Kentish countryside. The frugal can camp or repair to one of the nearby youth hostels.

If you're stuck for somewhere to stay, the **Visitor Centre** (see page 93) provides an accommodation booking service, though it's not free; if you want to avoid the charge, staff can give you a useful city brochure which has an extensive accommodation section at the back.

The Camping and Caravanning Club £ No need to be a member at this site, which is open all year. It's just over a mile due east of

the town centre, and accessible by bus or a half-hour walk.
There's Wi-Fi at the site, which has earned big ups from campers
for its friendliness and cleanliness.
ⓐ Bekesbourne Lane ☏ 01227 463216 (until 20.00)
ⓦ www.campingandcaravanningclub.co.uk ⓦ Bus: 13, 13A, 14

Canterbury Youth Hostel £ The official YHA hostel is housed
in an imposing Victorian villa 2 km (1¹/₄ miles) southeast of
the centre. Dorms sleep up to ten people, and there are
rooms for smaller groups, a single, double and triple. The
establishment is wheelchair accessible and has Wi-Fi. Prices
vary with the season. ⓐ Ellerslie, 54 New Dover Road ☏ 0845 371
9010 ⓦ www.yha.org.uk ⓔ canterbury@yha.org.uk ⓦ Bus: 15, 15A,
16, 23A, 89

Clare Ellen Guest House ££ Located in a quiet residential area
a short walk to the southwest of the centre, this family-run
guesthouse has seven rooms and a swimming pool. Internet
access is free and there's a good collection of leaflets to help you
plan your itinerary. Rates include breakfast, and discounts are
offered in low season. ⓐ 9 Victoria Road ☏ 01227 760205
ⓦ www.clareellenguesthouse.co.uk

Oriel Lodge ££ This detached Edwardian house, in the tranquil
residential neighbourhood of St Dunstan's, northwest of the
main action, has been converted into three one-bedroom self-
catering apartments. Laundry and Internet facilities are
provided. Let on a weekly, three- or four-night basis, it can offer
decent value if your Canterbury sojourn is longer than the norm.

ⓐ 3 Queens Avenue ⓣ 01227 462845 ⓦ www.oriel-lodge.co.uk
ⓔ info@oriel-lodge.co.uk

Victoria Hotel ££ Deep reds predominate at this classily furnished hotel in the northwest of town, which has 33 individually decorated rooms. Flat-screen televisions and Wi-Fi are among the modern amenities following recent refurbishment. Or spoil yourself with a four-poster bed and whirlpool. A family concern, the Victoria also has a carvery and bar. ⓐ 59 London Road ⓣ 01227 459333 ⓦ www.thevictoriahotel. co.uk ⓝ Bus: 27 (hourly service)

Wincheap Guest House ££ The hanging baskets that festoon this three-storey Victorian house, located minutes southwest of Canterbury East Railway Station, offer as warm a welcome as the owner, whose two decades in the hospitality trade reap him many returning customers. The six rooms vary in specifics; if the weather's nice, book the one with the patio. ⓐ 94 Wincheap ⓣ 01227 762309 ⓦ www.wincheapguesthouse.com ⓝ Train: Canterbury East

Ebury Hotel ££–£££ Set in verdant grounds and with an indoor swimming pool, the Ebury offers traditional accommodation (book a four-poster bed for a touch of old-school English elegance) in rooms sleeping up to four. On the same site, a short walk to the southeast of the old city, are self-catering cottages and serviced flats. There's free Wi-Fi and ample parking space. ⓐ 65–67 New Dover Road ⓣ 01227 768433 ⓦ www.ebury-hotel.co.uk ⓔ eburyhotel@googlemail.com

Thanington Hotel ££–£££ An indoor swimming pool, Georgian conservatory and courtyard garden are among the attractions of this place, which was built around 1785. The hotel, a brief walk to the southwest, has its own car park and free Wi-Fi access. The proprietors are particularly proud of their collection of single malt whiskies. ⓐ 140 Wincheap ⓣ 01227 453227 ⓦ www.thanington-hotel.co.uk

Magnolia House £££ This luxury B&B occupies a smart Georgian townhouse, tucked away in peaceful St Dunstan's. Books, magazines and board games are provided to amuse guests, and there is Internet access. Rooms, which are all en-suite, come with complimentary wine and mineral water, and the hotel can furnish you with corkscrews, ice and chillers should you wish to toast the occasion. ⓐ 36 St Dunstan's Terrace ⓣ 01227 765121 ⓦ www.magnoliahousecanterbury.co.uk

Sun Hotel £££ Practically unbeatable in terms of location, just minutes from the cathedral, this 15th-century inn's past guests include Kent traveller Charles Dickens. Since extensive refurbishment five years ago, the rooms have a more contemporary aspect, but most still contain historical highlights like four-poster beds, and the place is infused with Tudor charm. Pop down to the tea rooms for a cream tea. ⓐ 7–8 Sun Street ⓣ 01227 769700 ⓦ www.sunhotel-canterbury.co.uk

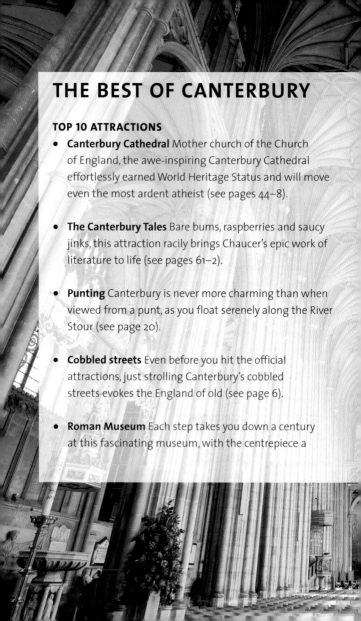

THE BEST OF CANTERBURY

TOP 10 ATTRACTIONS

- **Canterbury Cathedral** Mother church of the Church of England, the awe-inspiring Canterbury Cathedral effortlessly earned World Heritage Status and will move even the most ardent atheist (see pages 44–8).

- **The Canterbury Tales** Bare bums, raspberries and saucy jinks, this attraction racily brings Chaucer's epic work of literature to life (see pages 61–2).

- **Punting** Canterbury is never more charming than when viewed from a punt, as you float serenely along the River Stour (see page 20).

- **Cobbled streets** Even before you hit the official attractions, just strolling Canterbury's cobbled streets evokes the England of old (see page 6).

- **Roman Museum** Each step takes you down a century at this fascinating museum, with the centrepiece a two-millennia-old floor mosaic revealed by excavations occasioned by a German bomb (see pages 49–50).

- **Museum of Canterbury** From the Romans to Bagpuss via Joseph Conrad, the town's place in history is eclectically and imaginatively surveyed here (see pages 62–4).

- **Historical inns** Sup your ale and feast on hearty fare at one of the historical inns throughout the city (see page 16).

- **Canterbury Festival** Two October weeks of all manner of arty goings-on make up this famous cultural cornucopia (see page 9).

- **Gulbenkian Theatre & Cinema** From dark drama to cracking comedy and fancy film, your every cultural yearning will be sated here (see page 78).

- **Ancient religious architecture** At every juncture, history buffs will adore Canterbury and all it has on visual offer (see pages 44–8, 71–3).

Be stunned by the cathedral's architectural detail and historical significance

Suggested itineraries

HALF-DAY: CANTERBURY IN A HURRY

First stop must be the superb **Canterbury Cathedral**. The site could easily absorb more than an hour, perhaps two, but even if you're pushed for time you'll still want to allow at least 30 or 40 minutes. After you emerge, walk the streets around the cathedral, admiring the Tudor beams, quirky cobbles and distinctive boutiques. Next have a quick scoot round the **Museum of Canterbury**. From there you're a couple of minutes from **Water Lane**, the starting point for a glorious river punt – provided the weather is decent. You will disembark close to the many restaurants and cafés of **Castle Street**.

1 DAY: TIME TO SEE A LITTLE MORE

A full day means the previous suggestions can be approached less manically. Linger longer in the magnificent cathedral and extend your stroll. After the informative Museum of Canterbury, visit the resplendently kitsch **The Canterbury Tales**. Should the weather permit, enjoy a picnic lunch in **Dane John Gardens**, the **Franciscan Garden** or **West Gate Gardens**; otherwise, you're seldom far from a good café in the centre of Canterbury. If the night is yours as well, pop by the **Visitor Centre** to see if there's a concert or play that appeals, or visit a centuries-old pub.

2–3 DAYS: SHORT CITY BREAK

There is plenty more to see and do within the city walls. The fascinating and well-arranged **Roman Museum** definitely deserves a visit, as do **Eastbridge Hospital** and the **Norman**

Castle. Swing by the other notable city buildings, like **St George's Tower** and **West Gate Towers Museum**. You can now also venture outside the centre, with a foray to **St Augustine's Abbey** and **St Martin's Church**. Drama, drinking, comedy, clubbing or concert – your few days should afford you the chance to sample the nocturnal delights of Canterbury. For downtime, relax in the city's green spaces or head off for a coastal excursion.

LONGER: ENJOYING CANTERBURY TO THE FULL

East Kent is now your oyster. Make sure you take in a service at the cathedral. Punctuate your sightseeing with some retail therapy – perhaps a market – or the odd cinema outing. And head off for some traditional British seaside fun and water sports at **Herne Bay** or **Whitstable**.

◔ *If not a must-read, then definitely a must-see: The Canterbury Tales*

Something for nothing

Canterbury's historical architecture pervades the entire town centre, which makes a wander almost anywhere within the city walls a rewarding experience. The riverside walk along the Stour provides a good route for a sortie, provided it's a fine day.

Free attractions include **St Martin's Church**, the **Sidney Cooper Art Gallery**, the **Norman Castle** and **Greyfriars Chapel**. Canterbury's green spaces, such as **Dane John Gardens**, the **Franciscan Garden** and **West Gate Gardens**, can also be enjoyed at no financial outlay. The **Royal Museum and Art Gallery** will be free once it reopens in the spring of 2012.

Of course, it would be a pity to leave Canterbury without having visited its big hitters for budgetary reasons. One way around this is to attend a service at the cathedral, for which there is no admission fee. You would probably miss out on the crypt, but the nave is impressive enough, and a service would be a special experience. Another money-saving option if you're planning on doing a significant amount of sightseeing is the **Canterbury Attractions Passport**. Available from the **Visitor Centre** (see page 93) the ticket includes entry to the cathedral, St Augustine's Abbey, The Canterbury Tales and one city museum. So although it's neither free nor cheap, you do end up making quite a saving.

The **Gulbenkian** occasionally organises free or very cheap events, so it may be worth checking its website to see if anything is coming up. Both the Gulbenkian and **New Marlowe Theatre** have signed up for the Free Theatre Initiative, allocating some free tickets to those under 26.

When it rains

Canterbury's layout is a godsend on a wet day, with the majority of landmarks just a short scuttle from each other. The cathedral is an excellent destination if gloomy weather looks set to assert itself for some time. The **Museum of Canterbury** and **The Canterbury Tales** are very close, so make a good pair to do in a downpour, with a half-time dash between them.

Shopping enthusiasts could see out the storm at the **Marlowe Arcade** or in other stores at the **Whitefriars Centre**; if the outlook hasn't improved by the time you're all shopped out, the **Odeon Cinema** is just a couple of minutes away. Culture vultures should cab or bus it to the **Gulbenkian** on the university campus. Follow a matinee classic film with a potter round the gallery and an early dinner in the café-bar before an evening of comedy or drama. If a sudden shower catches you out, Canterbury has a plethora of inviting cafés where you can wait out the worst of the weather.

IT COULD BE WORSE...

However sodden your trip, it's nothing compared to the city's climate as depicted in Russell Hoban's dystopian science-fiction novel *Riddley Walker*. Rain is a near constant presence in the book's bleak, post-nuclear Canterbury, prompting the protagonist to muse, 'Theres rains and rains. This 1 wer coming down in a way as took the hart and hoap out of you.'

On arrival

ARRIVING

By air

The nearest airport to Canterbury is Kent International, 20 km
(12 miles) northeast of the city in Manston, Thanet. Its closest
station is Ramsgate, which is less than ten minutes away by
taxi (drivers wait immediately outside the terminal, or you can
pre-book). You can also take the 38 (sometimes 38A or 38B)
bus. From Ramsgate, fast trains reach Canterbury West in
20 minutes or so, departing about every half hour; if there are
no direct services, change at Minster. The train fare won't cost
you more than £5. The whole journey can also be made by bus,
changing on to the 8 or 9. If money is not an issue, take a taxi
all the way; pre-booked private cars are usually cheaper than
the hackney cabs that line up at ranks.

This corner of Kent is also within easy reach of the main
London airports. From Gatwick, the closest of the 'big two', expect
the drive to take upwards of one hour and 20 minutes, depending
on traffic. Starting out on the M25, go via the M26, M20 and M2,
after which you can follow the signs. If you're flying into
Heathrow, it will take a further 20 minutes since you'll be starting
out further round the M25, the London Orbital route. By train, the
journey takes two hours, sometimes two and a half, from
Gatwick, with at least one change in London. Two hours and
15 minutes is the likely journey time from Heathrow using a
combination of the Tube (underground train) and train, with two
changes in London. Though cheaper than the train, the coach trip
from Gatwick takes five or six hours and requires two changes. It's

a bit better from Heathrow: you'll be conveyed to Canterbury in three and a half to four hours, with just one change.

By rail

The city has two railway stations, Canterbury East and Canterbury West; the cathedral is equidistant from both. Somewhat oddly given the compass points in their names, they lie, respectively, to the south and north of the heart of town. The closest is Canterbury East, which is just outside the ring road that delineates the city centre, a little below Dane John Gardens. To reach the main action, cross the A28 or Pin Hill – an overpass goes from Station Road East so you don't need to dice with death on a busy A-road! There's a taxi rank outside, and a bus stop for the university round the corner.

Canterbury West, which was recently spruced up and made more accessible, is slightly further out, but the key attractions are still reachable on foot. Turn right on to Station Road West when you exit the station, then go left on to St Dunstan's Street, which will take you past West Gate and eventually on to the High Street. If the walk doesn't appeal, or you have luggage, there is a taxi rank outside. Buses go round, not through, the centre of Canterbury, so whichever station you pitch up at, you can't hop on a bus to the cathedral. But several routes circumnavigate the walled city, so if you're staying in a residential district there may be a useful bus service.

By road

Coach services unload their passengers even nearer to the midpoint than trains, adjacent to the Whitefriars Centre on

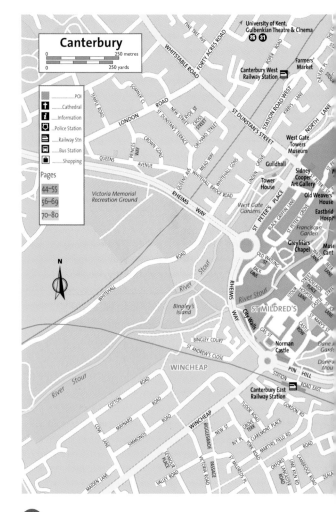

Canterbury

0 — 250 metres
0 — 250 yards

POI
Cathedral
Information
Police Station
Railway Stn
Bus Station
Shopping

Pages

44–55
56–69
70–80

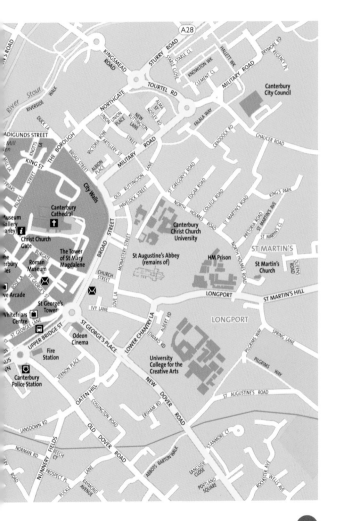

St George's Lane. You won't find a vast terminus, but the benches by the row of bays are undercover. From here, it is straightforward to reach the central sights.

If you're driving from London, you'll approach town on the M2, before branching off on to the A2. Following signs to Canterbury will take you via the A2050, A290 and A28, the latter forming part of the city's ring road. Much of the heart of town is pedestrianised and there are several one-way enclaves to compound the driver's headache. Depending on when you turn up you may also run into heavy traffic; parking too can be tricky. It may be better to abandon your vehicle either at your accommodation if it's in a peripheral zone – many of the B&Bs are in residential neighbourhoods that enjoy plenty of free parking – or use the inexpensive Park and Ride scheme, depositing your vehicle at New Dover Road, Sturry Road or Wincheap and switching to the bus (services every eight minutes or so throughout the day, Mon–Sat; usually no Sun service). Otherwise there are many official car parks around town. The council produces a leaflet with a map, detailing the different charges and operating times, while the general map issued by the Visitor Centre also features the car parks. In general, to avoid parking charges and traffic, try to park just outside the city walls and walk in.

FINDING YOUR FEET

Despite its city status, Canterbury's modest size means that it does not have that overwhelming metropolis atmosphere that can cow those not used to it, and most visitors quickly acclimatise. The centre is happily unblighted by drunken revelry. However, the newly arrived should bear in mind that the outlying residential areas, although leafy suburbia during the day, can feel creepy when deserted after dark. Though still generally safe, you may prefer not to amble around them alone, especially if you're female.

ORIENTATION

The city walls and the ring road that runs alongside them enclose the main business. This oval is bisected by Canterbury's

● *Enjoy a leisurely stroll along the beautiful River Stour*

foremost artery, which consists of St Peter's Street, the High Street and St George's Street. Taking the northern part of the oval, which is smaller than its southern counterpart, the eastern section is dominated by the unmistakable cathedral. However, the configuration of buildings obscures views of the huge church from much of town, so it's not a particularly useful landmark for orientation purposes unless you're right by it.

Another thoroughfare runs perpendicular to the High Street. Starting from the Norman Castle for pedestrian purposes (although it actually picks up where Wincheap leaves off), it starts as the obligingly named Castle Street, segues into St Margaret's Street, before intersecting with the High Street, after which it becomes Mercery Lane and finishes at Christ Church Gate, the cathedral entrance.

Canterburians are, by and large, an affable lot, and are usually obliging if you need directions. Some will even approach a bewildered tourist and offer assistance.

GETTING AROUND
On foot
Many of Canterbury's highlights are packed into a relatively small zone, so you may be able to walk everywhere without needing to use a car or public transport. The exception is the university, which is a bit of a trek once you've become accustomed to five- or ten-minute walks between places of interest.

By bus
If the hike does not appeal, hop on the bus. The Stagecoach-operated **Unibus** shuttles between the campus, train stations

and the city centre roughly every seven minutes during term-time. Useful services include the 4, 4A, 4X, 6, 6A, 6X and 27. If you're in town on an extended stay and are likely to be taking the bus fairly frequently, it might be worth picking up a multi-use pass.

If you're travelling to Canterbury by train, the Plusbus ticket offers good value. ⓦ www.plusbus.info

Stagecoach is the main bus operator in town; the timetables and route map are on its website. ⓦ www.stagecoachbus.com

⬥ *Canterbury is easy to navigate*

By bike

Canterbury's small enough to do on two wheels, and there are some cycle lanes. You might, however, struggle on the cobbles. If you didn't bring your own bike, there are a few rental outfits.

Canterbury Cycle Hire ⓐ The Goods Shed, Station Road West
ⓣ 01227 275156 ⓦ www.canterburycyclehire.com
Downland Cycles ⓐ The Malthouse, St Stephen's Road
ⓣ 01227 479643 ⓦ www.downlandcycles.co.uk

Car hire

Aside from nipping up to the university or shuttling back and forth between town and your accommodation if you have based yourself in one of the more far-flung suburbs, there's little need for your own set of wheels in Canterbury proper. However, a car would certainly come in handy for a jaunt to one of the coastal excursions featured in this guide, Whitstable and Herne Bay, or if Canterbury is just one stop on the itinerary of a wider Kentish or English tour.

Perhaps because of its compactness, the main national car-rental outfits do not have branches in Canterbury. However, there is an Avis outlet at Kent International Airport and Whitstable has a Sixt. You'll also find the odd independent car-hire firm in town.

Avis ⓦ www.avis.co.uk
Enterprise Car Hire ⓦ www.enterprise.co.uk
Kendall Cars ⓦ www.kendallcars.com
Sixt ⓦ www.sixt.co.uk

---

❶ *Intricate detail on the cathedral's façade*

THE CITY OF
Canterbury

Introduction to city areas

Parts one and two of the city areas guide deal with the 'oval': Canterbury city centre as delineated by the semicircle of medieval walls and the roads built where the remaining walls would stand were it not for the ravages of time. The first section is the area roughly to the north of the High Street. This zone is home to the flagship attraction, Canterbury Cathedral, and the Visitor Centre.

The second area is south of the High Street, including the main artery itself. A clutch of museums, a shopping centre, the starting point for punting, the castle and an attractive green space are all to be found in this part of town. Though divided in two for the purposes of this guide, it is easy to move between the two areas.

Third is the rather disparate grouping of attractions that fall outside the city walls, including St Augustine's Abbey and the nearby St Martin's Church, as well as the more remote Gulbenkian on the University of Kent campus. Some of the features that form part of the walls themselves are incorporated in this section.

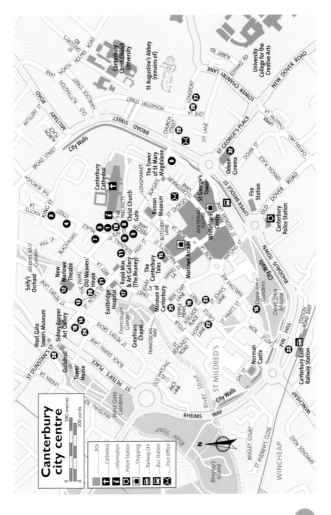

North of the High Street

Home to the city's pre-eminent attraction, the resplendent **Canterbury Cathedral**, many visitors make a beeline to this part of town, which oozes times past from every cobblestone. There's more history on tap at the **Roman Museum**, while even the shopping here has an olde-worlde feel; individual boutique establishments and ubiquitous corporate chains alike have designed their outlets sympathetically. The quarter is compact enough to get around on foot – indeed, you'll have to, since much of it is closed to traffic.

SIGHTS & ATTRACTIONS

Canterbury Cathedral

Part of a World Heritage Site and one of England's oldest and most prestigious churches, the history of this magnificent structure dates back to the turn of the 6th century, when the Pope deployed St Augustine to Kent to convert the natives and established a seat here. The existing edifice, however, has Norman origins and has been much amended since, giving it a Gothic aspect. From the outside, it is the Bell Harry Tower, which soars 72 m (326 ft) into the Kentish sky and houses a 17th-century bell that peals twice a day, that catches the eye. Yet much of the exterior detail, such as the statues carved into the masonry, is exquisite to behold. Architecture aficionados will be able to detect the juxtaposed styles of subsequent epochs.

However, it is the splendid interior that is the greatest attraction. Despite the number of tourists, the cathedral exudes a sense of sacredness and serenity. After adjusting to the tall, long Gothic proportions and vaulted ceiling, take time to admire the ornately engraved pulpit and the dazzling stained-glass windows, some of which date from the 12th and 13th centuries. Their tableaux often depict tales of both the Christian great and good and the ordinary folk of the time. The Martyrdom – the part where Thomas Becket met his end (see box, page 46) – is marked by a modern sculpture, and the Trinity Chapel houses the tomb of Henry IV. Arrows guide you around the cathedral from the nave down to the crypt. In low light, make your way around the numerous small chapels, tombs, plaques and candle collections. Devotee or day-tripper, discovering the crypt is

Stunning and imposing – Canterbury Cathedral

exceptionally moving. The centrepiece is the Treasury, but there is so much worthy of investigation – from 12th-century wall paintings to 21st-century touch screens – that if you are staying in Canterbury for a while, you may wish to pay a second visit.

MURDER IN THE CATHEDRAL

It is difficult to conceive that a place as peaceful as Canterbury Cathedral was once the scene of one of England's most brutal and notorious murders. Thomas Becket (born c. 1120) was raised and educated in relative affluence, the son of a wealthy London landlord. Taken into the employ of the Archbishop of Canterbury, he impressed his boss so much that the archbishop recommended him to Henry II, who made him chancellor. The two became firm friends: Becket was happy to share in his royal chum's kingly amusements and even housed Henry's son, a custom of the time. When Becket's old mentor died, Henry appointed him the new archbishop, intending to manipulate his loyal pal to keep the Church in its place. Unfortunately for him, Becket transformed himself from a pleasure-seeking courtier to a sober ascetic, and – to Henry's fury – set about staunchly defending the Church from the power-hungry monarch. The king's cry of 'Will no one rid me of this turbulent priest?' was understood as a royal command, and four hot-headed knights set out to do Henry's apparent bidding. Becket's gruesome dispatch in Canterbury Cathedral resulted in his canonisation.

Guided tours are available for an extra fee, departing from a marked pillar in the nave, and visitors can also pick up an audio guide. There's a welcome centre if you're curious to find out more, a well-stocked shop with a plethora of merchandise, and the exterior precincts are also worth a look. ⓐ The Precincts ☎ 01227 865222 ⓦ www.canterbury-cathedral.org ⓔ enquiries@canterbury-cathedral.org ⓛ Precincts 07.00–21.00; cathedral 09.00–17.30 Mon–Fri, 09.00–14.30 Sat, 12.30–14.30 Sun (summer); 09.00–17.00 Mon–Fri, 09.00–14.30 Sat, 12.00–14.30 Sun (winter); treasury 10.00–16.00 Mon–Sat, closed Sun (summer); 10.30–15.30 Mon–Sat, closed Sun (winter) ⓘ Last

◭ *A bronze Christ adorns Christ Church Gate*

entry 30 minutes before closing; sometimes closed for special events. Admission charge except for services

Christ Church Gate

This Norman gateway, the entrance to the cathedral, is an attraction in its own right. The tiered edifice was described by 17th-century antiquarian scholar William Somner as 'a very goodly, strong, and beautiful structure, and of excellent artifice'. It is hard to disagree. A retinue of small angels flanks the somewhat incongruously blue Christ, a 1991 addition. (A predecessor was destroyed in 1642 after being selected for target practice by disrespectful Parliamentarians, who were said to have 'discharged against it forty shot at the least, triumphing much when they did hit it in the head or face'.) Restoration has brought back much of its former glory – the line of elaborate crests directly above the archway are particularly fine. Don't forget to examine the ceiling while buying your cathedral ticket. **ⓐ** Junction of Burgate and St Margaret's Street

The Tower of St Mary Magdalene

Sole remainder of the church of the same name, which was pulled down in 1871 in an example of 19th-century health and safety philosophy, the tower was built in 1503. After the demolition, two of the 15th-century bells were sold to the Bishop of Madagascar. Housed inside it, behind a glass pane, is a baroque monument to the Whitfield family dating back to 1680. Patriarch John Whitfield is described as 'a liberal benefactor to the poor of this city'. **ⓐ** Burgate

CULTURE

Roman Museum

What have the Romans ever done for us? This and other questions you might have about our Latin forebears are answered at this absorbing museum. There would have been no museum had a German World War II bomb not exposed the remnants of a Roman house. Visitors descend – each step takes you down a hundred years – to an underground floor, the level of the ancient house. As well as the structure itself – replete with floor mosaic, some impressively forward-thinking under-floor heating, a market-place reconstruction and some modern-looking period glass – there's a map of how Durovernum Cantiacorum (the city's Latin moniker) would have looked, a Blitz display and some interactive gadgetry. Heaps of

⬥ *Soak up some history at the Roman Museum*

Roman bric-a-brac is on show and, unusually, visitors are welcome to handle it – archaeologists unearthed so many artefacts that they believe the excavation site was probably a town rubbish dump. ❸ Longmarket, Butchery Lane ❶ 01227 785575 ❿ www.canterbury.gov.uk ● 10.00–16.00 daily (last entry 15.00) ❶ Admission charge. Wheelchair access for one person at a time

RETAIL THERAPY

Art of Candles Family-run designer candle store, where shoppers can also watch the products being made. ❸ 51 Palace Street ❶ 01227 766007 ❿ www.artofcandles.co.uk ● 10.00–16.00 Tues–Fri, 10.00–17.00 Sat, closed Sun & Mon

Burgate Antiques Centre There is something of the Old Curiosity Shop about the Burgate Antiques Centre. A military mannequin is on hand to greet all comers at the door of this olde-worlde outlet, where military memorabilia and medals take their place on the shelves alongside prints, ornaments, toys, jewellery and other buys from yesteryear. ❸ 23a Palace Street ❶ 01227 456500 ● 10.00–17.00 Mon–Sat, closed Sun

Canterbury Cathedral Shop Manifold merchandise is on sale in the cathedral's retail wing. Much of it is religious, such as icons, DVDs and CDs of choral music, and there are also books (Chaucer is heavily represented). Upstairs is a gallery with more tomes, gifts, objets d'art and tapestries, including high-quality chocolates, mugs, tea towels, bags and games. The reverent background music provides a suitably devout setting for your browsing. ❸ Entrance on Burgate ☎ 01227 865300 ⓦ www.cathedral-enterprises.co.uk 🕐 09.30–17.30 Mon–Sat, 10.30–16.30 Sun

Fudge Kitchen Doing exactly what it says on the tin, Fudge Kitchen serves up fresh fudge, handmade on the premises, as well as some cakes. The shop also runs fudge-making sessions for two. ❸ 16 Sun Street ☎ 01227 479399 ⓦ www.fudgekitchen. co.uk 🕐 10.00–18.00 Mon–Sat, 10.00–17.00 Sun

King's Mile This royally named retail district starts at Guildhall Street, and runs through Palace Street (both pedestrianised) and the Borough to the far end of Northgate. It's a charming place for a spot of shopping, with the majority of outlets along its length being independent shops such as chichi jewellery boutiques, gourmet delis, fair-trade emporiums, art galleries, antiques stores, vintage clothing boutiques, old-fashioned sweet shops, arts and crafts outfits and their bohemian ilk, among more familiar high-street brands. ❸ From Guildhall Street to Northgate ⓦ www.thekingsmile.com

Madame Oiseau Exquisite homemade confectionery is so beautifully presented here that only the most disciplined will be able to walk by this place and not be tempted. Demonstrations of chocolate making are sometimes held. ❸ 8 The Borough ☎ 01227 452222 ⓦ www.madame-oiseau.com ✉ contact@madame-oiseau.com 🕐 10.00–17.30 Mon–Sat, closed Sun

...t over the road ...leaning forward, trying to see who was passing on the narrow pavement below... " Charles Dickens, 1849

formerly the
Old King's School Shop
circa 1647

KING'S ENGLISH

⬥ *Don't miss fascinating old buildings like this one on the King's Mile*

Siesta This craft store's hippie, ethical ethos is evident in every item on sale, from the musical instruments and Tibetan incense to the ethnic wooden elephants. The fair-trade emporium is also a meeting point for the bohemian community, with leaflets advertising yoga, tai chi, concerts and environmental happenings posted on the wall. ⓐ 1 Palace Street ⓣ 01227 464614 ⓦ www.siestacrafts.co.uk ⓛ 09.30–17.30 Mon–Fri, 09.30–18.00 Sat, 10.30–16.30 Sun

TAKING A BREAK

Caffe Venezia £–££ ❶ As well as the pizza and pasta that the name implies, this reasonably priced eatery will take care of you throughout the day serving staples like breakfasts, sandwiches, jacket potatoes and cream teas. ❸ 60–61 Palace Street ❶ 01227 787786 Ⓦ www.caffevenezia.co.uk ⓔ info@caffevenezia.co.uk Ⓛ 08.30–17.30 Mon–Sat, 09.00–16.30 Sun; brasserie menu 18.15–22.00 Fri & Sat

22 ££ ❷ The philosophy that 'simplicity is the ultimate sophistication' seems to prevail at 22, which serves fresh food fashioned from local ingredients under the slogan 'food from the heart, not from the freezer'. ❸ 22 Palace Street ❶ 01227 479500 Ⓦ www.22canterbury.co.uk Ⓛ 09.00–16.30 Mon–Sat, closed Sun

Chambers of Canterbury ££ ❸ Another historic establishment (read all about it on the wall), this espresso bar is not the cheapest place to eat and drink, but the cheery orange décor, friendly ambience and free Wi-Fi are compensations. ❸ 59 Palace Street ❶ 01227 464285 Ⓛ 10.00–18.00 Mon–Fri, 09.00–18.00 Sat, 10.00–17.00 Sun & bank holidays

Cucina Caraccio ££ ❹ Smart and friendly, this café is a perfect place to stop for a top-quality, bona-fide Italian coffee and a slice of cake, or take your pick from an array of other fare. ❸ 15 Palace Street ❶ 01227 472401 Ⓛ 09.30–16.30 Tues–Fri, 09.30–16.00 Sat, closed Sun & Mon

Ferns ££ ❺ Up the stairs to the left of the Visitor Centre, this friendly joint is surprisingly peaceful considering its central location. Traditional treats such as a full English breakfast, ploughman's lunch and afternoon tea for two can be rounded off nicely with one of the cakes from the display. ⓐ 12–13 Sun Street ⓣ 01227 781885 ⓛ 09.30–16.00 Mon–Fri, 09.30–17.00 Sat, 11.00–16.00 Sun

The Moat Tea Rooms ££ ❻ Welcoming, family-run tea rooms that are big on tradition and service. There's a full range of lunches such as sandwiches, salads and jackets, and the selection of desserts, cakes and other baked goodies – displayed tantalisingly in the window – is to die for. ⓐ 67 Burgate ⓣ 01227 784514 ⓦ www.moattearooms.co.uk ⓛ 09.00–18.00 Mon–Fri, 08.00–18.00 Sat, 11.00–17.00 Sun

Pastry Patisserie ££ ❼ It is the cakes – beguilingly flaunted at the counter – that earn rave reviews for this place. The homemade ice cream goes down quite well too. ⓐ 2 Palace Street ⓣ 01227 450146 ⓛ 09.00–18.00 Mon–Sat, closed Sun

Shake Shed ££ ❽ A phenomenal assortment of milkshakes and smoothies, as well as waffles, paninis, nachos and cakes for the more indulgent consumer. ⓐ 18 Sun Street ⓣ 01227 764378 ⓛ 09.30–18.00 Mon–Sat, 10.30–17.00 Sun

Sun Hotel Crêperie ££ ❾ The building – which dates from 1503 – may be old but the concept is contemporary at this pancake house. Sweet and savoury flavours include ratatouille, bacon

and brie, and Grand Marnier with fresh oranges. ⓐ 7–8 Sun
Street ⓣ 01227 769700 ⓦ www.sunhotel-canterbury.co.uk
ⓛ Crêperie 10.00–17.00 daily; bar 10.00–22.00 daily

Deeson's British Restaurant ££–£££ ⑩ Trumpeting its local,
seasonal and free-range ethos, classy Deeson's is a proud
purveyor of Kentish and regional cuisine, its menu featuring
such highlights as partridge, oysters, hake and pan-roasted loin
of Sussex steer beef. ⓐ 25–26 Sun Street ⓣ 01227 767854
ⓛ 12.00–16.00, 18.00–22.00 Mon–Sat, 12.00–16.00 Sun

Manolis Taverna ££–£££ ⑪ Established 20 years ago, this Greek-
owned and run traditional taverna is as authentically Hellenic
as Zorba and plate smashing. From calamari to moussaka to the
national salad, it's all there, and you can lubricate proceedings
with a glass of ouzo. ⓐ 10 Guildhall Street ⓣ 01227 769189
ⓦ www.manolistaverna.co.uk ⓛ 12.00–14.30, 18.00–22.00 Mon,
12.00–14.30, 18.00–22.30 Tues–Sat, closed Sun

AFTER DARK

New Marlowe Theatre ⑫ The New Marlowe Theatre is due to
open towards the end of 2011 with a wide-ranging programme of
events, from drama and music to comedy and pantomime. In the
meantime, the theatre's performances are being farmed out to
other local venues; consult the website for what's happening
where. The Visitor Centre has a ticket desk for the theatre.
ⓐ The Friars ⓣ 01227 378116 ⓦ www.newmarlowetheatre.org.uk
ⓔ marlowetheatre@canterbury.gov.uk

South of the High Street

Although the cathedral is the main tourist hub, there is plenty to occupy you on the other side of the High Street. Several historical buildings of note and museums are situated here, as well as a handy starting point for a punt along the river. On top of all that are myriad places to buy refreshments, plus the main shopping centre.

While there are fewer pedestrianised streets here, there are still enough one-way roads to flummox the out-of-town motorist, and driving around the area is probably more trouble than it's worth. Even the furthest two points included in this section are not prohibitively far apart for the walker, and there are plenty of places to stop for a refreshing tea or snack if you find yourself beginning to flag.

SIGHTS & ATTRACTIONS

Dane John Gardens

In use since at least the 12th century, this popular green space was laid out in its present form in 1790. Dotting the gardens are various features, including a fountain, sundial and bandstand. Perhaps the most striking monument is the restored **Boer War Memorial**, solemnly commemorating the fallen of several Kent units. On a more upbeat note, there's a play area for children, and energetic park-goers can scale the demanding **Dane John Mound**, atop which stands another monument, this time in honour of the alderman who presented the gardens to the people of Canterbury in the 18th century. Your ascent will also be rewarded with some fine city views. A kiosk sells refreshments throughout the year, and the gardens also host cultural events in season. ⓐ Watling Street ⓦ www.canterbury.co.uk ⓛ 24 hours

Eastbridge Hospital

This might sound an unlikely tourist attraction, but the word 'hospital' here is used in its archaic sense to mean a place of hospitality. Since being founded in the 12th century, it has provided accommodation and aid to the poorest pilgrims, soldiers, local societies and schoolchildren. For the past four centuries, it has also housed elderly people. A tour takes in the undercroft and its atmospheric Gothic arches, where the penniless pilgrims would have slept, the refectory – a highlight of which is the 13th-century mural – and the pilgrims' and

◯ Rest and find some solace at the Eastbridge Hospital

⬤ *Admire the medieval architecture of Greyfriars Chapel*

chantry chapels. The latter are still used for services, which visitors are welcome to attend. ⓐ 25 High Street ⓣ 01227 471688 ⓦ www.eastbridgehospital.org.uk ⓔ info@eastbridgehospital.org.uk ⓛ 10.00–17.00 Mon–Sat, closed Sun ⓘ Admission charge

Greyfriars Chapel and the Franciscan Garden

It's not as big as Dane John, but the Franciscan Garden is another peaceful green space in the centre of town. The river runs through it, and a weeping willow adds to the calm. The striking chapel is the sole surviving vestige of the first English Franciscan friary, which dates back to the 13th century. A small exhibition on the lower floor elucidates the history. ⓐ Franciscan Way ⓣ 01227 471688 ⓦ www.eastbridgehospital.org.uk ⓛ Chapel 14.00–16.00 Mon–Sat, closed Sun (Easter–end Sept); gardens 10.00–17.00 (summer); 10.00–dusk (winter)

Norman Castle

Once forming a trio with counterparts in Rochester and Dover as the original Royal castles of Kent, the first edifice around this area was a motte-and-bailey construction, built soon after the Battle of Hastings in 1066 to safeguard the key London to Dover road. Stones replaced wood during the reign of Henry I, and in the 13th century the place became a jail. Prisoners were incarcerated in the basement, where their view of the outside world was through three narrow slit windows; however, for much of the time the inmates were shackled in the yard, and permitted to beg for money and food from charitable passers-by. The remaining part of the keep conveys a decent idea of what

● *Walk in the footsteps of William the Conqueror at the Norman Castle*

the castle must have looked like, and exploration of the site is diverting. ⓐ Castle Street, go down Gas Street and turn left to reach the entrance ⓦ www.canterbury.co.uk ⓛ 08.00–dusk

Old Weavers' House

Set alongside the river, in which the reflection of its back wall provides an iconic Canterbury image, the half-timbered Old Weavers' House is so-named for the Flemish and Huguenot Weavers, continental Protestants who quit their native lands to escape religious persecution and earned the royal right to carry out their skilled trade on the premises. This 500-year-old house now serves as a restaurant. On the river side of the building is a replica ducking stool. ⓐ 3 St Peter's Street

CULTURE

The Canterbury Tales

Yes, it's kitschy, but this highly entertaining attraction is a Canterbury must-see. The converted Anglo-Saxon building of St Margaret's Church now abounds with the sights, sounds and smells of 14th-century England, as rendered by Chaucer in his eponymous story collection (see box, page 62). With an audio guide, you move from one scene to another, as animated Chaucerian figures play out truncated versions of the five tales you're hearing, which have been re-recorded in modern-day language without sacrificing any of the poet's irreverence – bare

◆ *One of Canterbury's most photographed buildings: the Old Weavers' House*

buttocks emerge from a window, there are shenanigans aplenty and the Miller lets out a raspberry. It's all very well done and great fun; the effects are excellent. ⓐ St Margaret's Street ⓣ 01227 479227 ⓦ www.canterburytales.org.uk ⓛ 10.00–17.00 daily (Mar–June); 09.30–17.00 daily (July & Aug); 10.00–17.00 daily (Sept & Oct); 10.00–16.30 daily (Nov–Feb) ⓘ Admission charge

Museum of Canterbury

This building, now the municipal museum, has an extraordinarily diverse history – since 1180 it has served as a minister's home, poor priests' hospital, church school, prison, Victorian workhouse, World War II ambulance station and family planning clinic. The museum employs a time-walk concept, with rooms

THE CANTERBURY TALES

One of the most important entries in the English canon, Geoffrey Chaucer's rich, seminal and wickedly funny epic skewers human foibles, the Church and the hypocrisy of the upper classes, while providing a page-turning read that would have delighted its audience with its irreverence and ribaldry. The premise is simple: en route to Canterbury a diverse group of pilgrims agree to participate in a storytelling competition to provide diversion. The vivid tales, related by such unforgettable narrators as the licentious Wife of Bath and the lecherous Miller, are quite possibly the greatest work of poetry in the English language.

○ *Learn about the city at the Museum of Canterbury*

chronologically charting Durovernum Cantiacorum's journey to contemporary Canterbury, up to about the 1960s. It's a truly mixed bag. There's Invicta, said to be the first passenger train in the world, which valiantly shuttled intrepid Kentish folk between Whitstable and Canterbury in 1830, a display on 'Pagan Canterbury' and a beamed Great Hall. A riveting historical tapestry relates the story of Thomas Becket, and there are lively information panels on subjects such as 'death and disease'. Particularly fun are rooms devoted to children's favourites Rupert the Bear (devised by local lady Mary Tourtel) and Bagpuss, Noggin the Nog and other characters created by fellow Canterburian Oliver Postgate. From far away, both artistically and geographically, the study of Polish-born novelist Joseph Conrad, who lived and died in the city, is reproduced. From the sombre – the murder of Becket – to the silly – Sir Paul McCartney's Frog Chorus – the entire museum is a joy. The temporary art gallery is currently closed for long-term refurbishment. ⓐ Stour Street
ⓣ 01227 475202 ⓦ www.canterbury-museums.co.uk
ⓛ 11.00–16.00 Mon–Sat, closed Sun (Oct–May); 11.00–16.00 Mon–Sat, 13.30–16.00 Sun (June–Sept) ⓘ Admission charge

Royal Museum & Art Gallery (the Beaney)
This attraction includes the area's major visual arts space, antiquities and other artefacts in the main museum, and various militaria in the Buffs Gallery. It is due to reopen in spring 2012 after extensive renovation. Along with the New Marlowe Theatre the Beaney, as it is sometimes known, is intended to form a thriving cultural quarter. ⓐ High Street ⓣ 01227 452747
ⓦ www.canterbury.gov.uk ⓔ museums@canterbury.gov.uk

Sidney Cooper Art Gallery

A Canterbury Christ Church University concern, the Sidney Cooper's mission is to profile 'high-quality work rooted in a sense of tradition/the aesthetic'. Lectures and workshops are held alongside innovative and interactive temporary exhibitions. Upmarket art books are on sale in the small shop. ⓐ St Peter's Street ⓣ 01227 453267 ⓦ www. canterbury.ac.uk/sidney-cooper ⓛ 11.00–17.30 Tues–Fri, 12.00–17.30 Sat, closed Sun & Mon ⓘ Exhibitions free but charges are made for some workshops

RETAIL THERAPY

The Canterbury Tales Shop If the enjoyable The Canterbury Tales attraction has encouraged you to investigate the text itself, many tomes and DVDs on the great man are on sale in the attached shop. There are also plenty of non-Chaucerian products, such as cookies, rock, fudge, sweets and West-Country mead, artwork, postcards, posters, plates, jewellery and mugs. ⓐ St Margaret's Street ⓣ 01227 479227 ⓦ www.canterburytales.org.uk ⓛ 10.00–17.00 daily (Mar–June); 09.30–17.00 daily (July & Aug); 10.00–17.00 daily (Sept & Oct); 10.00–16.30 daily (Nov–Feb)

The Chaucer Bookshop If sauntering along the cobblestones once trodden by Christopher Marlowe and exploring the locations that inspired Chaucer and T S Eliot to put pen (or quill) to paper has awakened literary leanings in you, visit the Chaucer Bookshop. Now over half a century old, this atmospheric bibliophile's paradise stocks voluminous volumes on art, architecture, history, English literature, topography, travel, food and wine, railways, and more. You can also purchase cards here. ⓐ 6–7 Beer Cart Lane ① 01227 453912 ⓦ www.chaucer-bookshop.co.uk ⓛ 10.00–17.00 Mon–Sat, closed Sun

Mr Simms Your teeth won't thank you but your nostalgia glands will certainly savour this 'olde sweet shoppe'. Old-school jars line the walls, brimming with sugary treats such as Tia Maria truffles, rhubarb and custard sweets and jellybeans. Wham Bars and Dip Dabs also flank the route of this trip down confectionery's memory lane. ⓐ 1 High Street ① 01227 768666 ⓛ 09.30–18.00 Mon–Fri, 09.00–19.00 Sat, 11.00–17.00 Sun

Museum of Canterbury Shop Canterbury paraphernalia abounds here. If the Rupert or Bagpuss exhibitions have pushed your nostalgia buttons, take home a toy and relive your childhood. ⓐ Stour Street ① 01227 475202 ⓦ www.canterbury-museums.co.uk ⓛ 11.00–about 16.30 Mon–Sat, closed Sun (Oct–May); 11.00–about 16.30 Mon–Sat, 13.30–about 16.30 Sun (June–Sept)

Whitefriars Centre Millions of pounds were lavished on this shopping centre, the result of which is an agreeable retail district. The centre is anchored by **Fenwick** (ⓦ www.fenwick.co.uk ⓛ 09.00–17.30 Mon–Wed & Fri, 09.00–19.00 Thur, 09.00–18.00 Sat, 11.00–17.00 Sun), Canterbury's flagship department store, and most other major fashion chains also have outlets here. There's a food market in **Whitefriars Square** on the second and last Friday of the month, where the provisions include upmarket bread, cake, cheese, game, preserves, seafood, vegetables and the like. ⓐ Off St George's Street ⓦ www.whitefriars-canterbury.co.uk

TAKING A BREAK

A E Barrow & Sons £ ⓭ Waitresses dressed in domestic maids' uniforms set the tone at this old-fashioned parlour with a highly tempting window display. ⓐ 7 St Peter's Street ⓣ 01227 780742 ⓛ 08.30–17.00 Mon–Sat, closed Sun

Andy 88 Café £ ⓮ It's not Canterbury's glitziest establishment, but Andy 88's crêpes, salads, jackets and burgers will fill a hole without making one in your wallet. ⓐ 48 St Peter's Street ⓣ 01227 786888 ⓔ andy_lin@hotmail.co.uk ⓛ 07.00–17.00 Mon–Sat, 09.00–16.00 Sun ⓘ No toilet; customers can use next door's

City Fish Bar £ ⓯ The time-honoured British culinary staple of fish 'n' chips gets rave reviews at this unpretentious eatery. Some outside tables in summer. ⓐ 30 St Margaret's Street ⓣ 01227 760873 ⓛ 10.00–19.00 Mon–Sat, closed Sun

Dane John Gardens Tea Room £ ⓰ This small kiosk purveys an economically priced selection of park-appropriate foodstuffs, such as hot drinks, bacon rolls, hot dogs, baguettes and sandwiches. ⓐ Dane John Gardens ⓣ 01227 378100 ⓛ 09.30–around 18.00 (summer); 10.00–16.00 (winter)

Boho Café Bar ££ ⓱ Colour and atmosphere radiate from this quirky little gem on the High Street. The menu is as eclectic as the vibe, with dishes from all over the world, such as falafel, mussels and burgers, competing for your favour. ⓐ 27 High Street ❶ 01227 458931 ⏱ 09.00–17.00 Mon, 09.00–21.00 Tues–Sat, 10.00–17.00 Sun

Café St Pierre ££ ⑱ Bistro chic emanates from Café St Pierre. It's not cheap, but the quality of the filled baguettes, hot snacks, pastries and drinks and the warmth of the welcome are worth the price. ⓐ 41 St Peter's Street ❶ 01227 456791 ⏱ 08.00–18.00 Mon–Sat, 09.00–17.30 Sun

Lilford Gallery Café ££ ⑲ Sate your cultural appetite as well as your hunger at this gallery-cum-café. Light lunches, sandwiches, cakes or one of the daily specials can be topped off with an Illy coffee. ⓐ 76a Castle Street ❶ 01227 766616 ⓦ www.lilford gallery.com ⏱ 10.00–16.30 Mon–Sat, closed Sun

Little Italy ££ ⑳ The Tudor building and smart interior provide a welcoming ambience for the consumption of Italian entrées such as house signature dish *zuppa di pesce alla Genovese*. ⓐ 3 St Peter's Street ❶ 01227 472232 ⓦ www.littleitaly canterbury.com ⏱ 11.00–22.30 daily

Old Weavers' House ££ ㉑ Low ceilings and beams characterise this eatery, which occupies one of Canterbury's flagship buildings. Classic English dishes, like roast lamb, mingle with international favourites, such as pasta and stir fry, on the good-value menu. ⓐ 1–3 St Peter's Street ❶ 01227 464660 ⓦ www.weaversrestaurant.co.uk ⏱ 11.00–23.00 daily

Pinocchio's ££ ㉒ Settle yourself in the cosily traditional interior, get comfortable and check out the specials board. Whether you plump for pizza, pasta, meat or fish, it's certain to be delectable, and the young staff are friendly and attentive. ❷ 64 Castle Street ❶ 01227 457538 ❿ www.pinocchios canterbury.com ❸ 12.00–15.00, 18.00–22.30 Mon–Sat, 12.00–15.00 Sun

Saffron Café ££ ㉓ Follow the homemade soup with a well-priced main course or wrap, or knock back a delicious smoothie. ❷ 9 Castle Street, corner with St John's Lane ❶ 01227 780005 ❿ www. saffroncafe.co.uk ❸ 07.30–16.00 Mon–Sat, 08.30–15.00 Sun

Tacos Locos ££–£££ ㉔ Tortillas, nachos, tacos, fajitas and tapas are among the spicy Mexi-canapés, though the tequila, iced tea, sangria and margarita are probably of equal interest to the up-for-it clientele. Olé! ❷ 45 St Peter's Street ❶ 01227 379330 ❿ www.tacoslocos.co.uk ❸ 11.30–23.00 daily

AFTER DARK

Beer Cart Arms ㉕ Live music and DJs on some nights, but the theme changes every evening, so check ahead. ❷ 14–15 Beer Cart Lane ❶ 01227 826901 ❸ 17.00–23.00 Mon–Thur, 17.00–01.00 Fri, 12.00–01.00 Sat, 12.00–23.30 Sun ❶ Entry charge on some nights

Outside the city walls

Though many tourists might consider Canterbury as being
synonymous with the old city (the part within the medieval
walls), two-thirds of its World Heritage Site in fact lies outside
this central oval. As well as the ancient religious edifices of
St Augustine's Abbey and St Martin's Church, the town beyond
the wall is home to the Gulbenkian, a Canterbury cultural
powerhouse. While sites like the two World Heritage churches
and some of the architecture close to the walls can be seen on
foot, the Gulbenkian, on the university campus, is more remote.
Unless you're content to take a rather long walk, a bus or cab
could come in handy here.

◔ *The River Stour flows right through the historic city centre and beyond*

SIGHTS & ATTRACTIONS

River Stour

Meandering through Canterbury, the Kentish waterway pops up in each of the three areas covered in the main section of the guide, but is listed here because much of the riverside walk is outside the city walls. The walk consists of a network of pathways and gardens that lie alongside the babbling section of the Stour. Highlights include sculptures by the Causeway that were fashioned from trees that fell victim to a big storm in 1998, a wildflower meadow and some charmingly bucolic historic watermills. Solly's Orchard (ⓐ St Peter's Lane ⓛ Approximately early morning–dusk) is a popular riverside picnic spot.

St Augustine's Abbey

St Augustine's Abbey was built outside the city centre for good cause: Christian tradition banned burials within the walls. The original Saxon church that stood on the site, built at the behest of the monk Augustine, came down in Norman times, and the abbey was erected in its stead. Additions and tinkering continued over the following centuries, until Henry VIII's Dissolution of the Monasteries in the 1530s, after which parts of the abbey were dismantled and the remainder converted to a royal residence for Anne of Cleves, Henry's fourth wife. Though it was comparable to the cathedral at its architectural zenith, it has not fared so well since, but there is still plenty to see, and an audio guide can help you build up a fuller impression of what the place would have been like. ⓐ Monastery Street ⓣ 0870 333 1181 ⓦ www.english-heritage.org.uk ⓛ 10.00–17.00

Wed–Sun, closed Mon & Tues (Apr–June); 10.00–18.00 daily (July & Aug); 10.00–17.00 Sat & Sun, closed Mon–Fri (Sept–Oct); 10.00–16.00 Sat & Sun, closed Mon–Fri (Nov–Mar) ❶ Last admission 30 minutes before closing. Admission charge

St Martin's Church

Part of the World Heritage trilogy along with Canterbury Cathedral and the nearer St Augustine's Abbey, St Martin's Church holds the notable distinction of being the oldest parish church in the English-speaking world in continuous use. It has

⬤ *Marvel at the ruins of St Augustine's Abbey*

served as a place of worship since 580, when it was converted from a Roman building that had fallen into disuse and the original chapel was extended at the behest of Augustine. A tower was installed in the Middle Ages, and other parts of the site were amended or added over the intervening centuries – most of the glass and the organ, for example, are Victorian. However, some very early features are still visible: the font goes back to late Saxon or early Norman times, while the oldest part is by the first steps. A guide is always present to point out noteworthy aspects, such as the east window, which depicts Augustine baptising Æthelberht, and a statue of his wife, Queen Bertha of Kent. You can also explore with the aid of a tour leaflet. As well as visiting the church itself, leave time to wander outside in the cemetery (Rupert the Bear creator Mary Tourtel is buried here; her grave plus those of other notables are also marked on a leaflet). The singular atmosphere brought about by long-forgotten gravestones, some tilting at bizarre angles, is a peculiarly peaceful, quintessentially English experience.

ⓐ North Holmes Road, close to junction with Longport and St Martin's Hill ☎ 01227 453469 or 01227 768072 ⓦ www.martin paul.org ⓛ Usually Tues, Thur, Sat 11.00–16.00, closed Mon, Wed, Fri, Sun (Apr–Sept); Tues, Thur, Sat 11.00–15.00, closed Mon, Wed, Fri, Sun (Oct–Mar); possibly other times if you call in advance ⓘ Difficult to approach by car, so try to park nearby

West Gate Gardens

Another pretty green space, West Gate Gardens lie just outside the ring road where the medieval wall once stood. Extending over 4.5 hectares (11 acres), they have served as a public space since the Middle Ages. The presence of the River Stour, replete with swans, ducks and moorhens, adds to the bucolic niceness, and the gardens are popular with locals stopping off for a sit-down on one of the benches. Features include the attractive, crest-bearing Tower House. Built on Roman foundations from 14th-century reconstructed flint, it houses the Lord Mayor of Canterbury's administrative office and is not open to the public; the Guildhall, formerly the 1380 Church of the Holy Cross of Canterbury, is likewise closed to the public. Top of the botanic attributes is the Oriental Plane tree, which is two centuries old and 7.6 m (25 ft) wide. The Norman archway and other medieval vestiges that adorn the space were probably snaffled by resourceful Victorians from St Augustine's Abbey. The gardens have been earmarked for lottery funding so they may see a makeover shortly. ⓐ Westgate Grove, next to West Gate Towers ⏰ Dawn–dusk, daily

West Gate Towers Museum

Standing sentinel over the London road for six centuries is this well-preserved and striking gateway, built as a fortification against the French in the Hundred Years' War (1337–1453). The largest – and one of the finest – surviving city gates in the country, it towers 18 m (60 ft) above the pedestrians and pilgrims who have streamed back and forth underneath since 1380. Of course, the structure was not built for modern traffic and watching a double-decker bus gingerly negotiate its passage through is quite something. The gate has a suitably chequered history, having at various times been adorned with the severed head of rebel leader Bluebeard the Hermit, besieged

○ Relive Canterbury's turbulent history at the West Gate Towers Museum

and set alight by Parliamentarians and turned into a prison (for Canterbury criminals, Kentish felons being incarcerated in the Norman Castle). Today West Gate is rather calmer. Home to a museum, the former cells and guards' quarters host weaponry, replica armour for today's young knights to try on and some Magna Carta maquettes. Both the original cells and 'murder holes' from which West Gate guardians could dump boiling oil and cannon balls on the heads of the enemies below are visible; the less bloodthirsty can enjoy the holes for their city views. ❸ St Peters Street ❶ 11.00–12.30, 13.30–15.30 Sat only ❶ Admission charge; entrance under archway, no wheelchair access

RETAIL THERAPY

Farmers' Market Said to be Britain's first permanent farmers' market, this laudable emporium sells a vast range of seasonal fresh produce and locally made foodstuffs. There's also a restaurant on site (The Goods Shed, next to the station), where you can take a hiatus from the grocery-fest and enjoy a spot of lunch. ❸ Station Road West ❶ 01227 459153 ❶ www. thegoodsshed.net ❶ 09.00–19.00 Tues–Sat, 10.00–16.00 Sun, closed Mon

TAKING A BREAK

The eateries outside the city walls tend to be less expensive and more unassuming than those inside, since they don't pick up as much tourist trade.

Gulbenkian £ 26 As well as an appetising international menu, which varies with the time of day but suits the student budget, this theatre venue also stages comedy nights and concerts. Booking a table is recommended, especially on big performance nights. ❸ University of Kent campus, off Hackington Road ☏ 01227 769075 ⓦ www.kent.ac.uk/gulbenkian ⏰ Normally 08.00–22.00 Mon–Fri, 17.00–22.00 Sat, closed Sun ⓝ Bus: 4, 4A, 6, 6A, 24, 26A, Unibuses ❶ Opening times may vary depending on performances

Longport Café £ 27 This brightly decorated traditional British café and sandwich bar offers an extensive, cheap and cheerful menu. Credit cards accepted. ❸ 9 Longport ☏ 01227 451055 ⏰ 08.00–17.00 Mon–Sat, 09.00–16.00 Sun

Royal Inn £ 28 A plethora of Chinese choices, including indulgences such as lobster, are yours for the asking at the Royal Inn. Occupying a Georgian townhouse, the dining room is smart, with a lot of pine and florid decor. ❸ 1–2 Longport ☏ 01227 453063 ⏰ 12.00–14.00, 17.30–23.00 Tues–Thur, 12.00–14.00, 17.30–23.30 Fri & Sat, 17.30–23.00 Sun, closed Mon

Azouma £–££ 29 Reminiscent more of casbah than Canterbury, Azouma rustles up delicious Arabic and Mediterranean food and stages a weekly belly-dancing show. The rich reds, wooden furniture and brightly coloured cushions all radiate a Middle Eastern atmosphere, perfect for taking a relaxing break from all the sightseeing. A lunch buffet and a three-course set menu make economic choices. ❸ 4 Church Street ☏ 01227 760076

Ⓦ www.azouma.co.uk Ⓛ 12.00–14.30, 18.00–23.00 Mon–Fri,
12.00–24.00 Sat, 12.00–22.00 Sun

Café des Amis du Mexique ££–£££ Ⓕ It's worth venturing
outside the city walls to dine at this place, whose devotees
include actor Orlando Bloom. Bright yellow walls bedecked by
funky pictures, lively Latin American music and a convivial
Mexican ambience supply the ideal environs for polishing off
the fajitas, salsa and other favourites. If your palate can take
the heat, try a fiendishly hot habanero chilli. Ⓐ 95 St Dunstan's
Street Ⓣ 01227 464390 Ⓦ www.cafedez.com Ⓛ 12.00–22.00
Mon–Thur, 12.00–22.30 Fri & Sat, 12.00–21.30 Sun

AFTER DARK

ARTS VENUES
Gulbenkian Theatre & Cinema Ⓕ Its capacity for an audience of
340 viewers lends the Gulbenkian an intimate feel, ideal for
drama and the regular comedy nights it hosts. On the melodic
menu are world music, jazz, folk and classical, and there's an
art gallery. The venue channels the talents of professionals,
amateurs and students alike. A civilised cinema broadcasts a
selection of the more intelligent mainstream output plus classic
film and other arty offerings. Tickets can be booked online, by
phone or in person. Ⓐ University of Kent campus, off Hackington
Road Ⓣ 01227 769075 Ⓦ www.kent.ac.uk/gulbenkian Ⓛ Booking
office: 11.00–10 minutes after last event begins Mon–Sat, 14.00–
10 minutes after last event begins Sun Ⓝ Bus: 4, 4A, 6, 6A, 24,
26A, Unibuses

◆ *Get cultured at the Gulbenkian Theatre & Cinema*

Odeon Cinema 🕲 Frequent showings throughout the day of the latest major releases. ⓐ 43–45 St George's Place ⓣ 0871 224 4007 ⓦ www.odeon.co.uk

NIGHTCLUBS

Club Chemistry 🕲 Three different nightspots – the Bizz, the Works and Baa Bars – reopened in late 2010 as one super-venue. The eclectic music policy encompasses chart, party, dance, funky house, garage, dub-step, R&B, hip hop, dancehall and urban. ⓐ Station Road East ⓣ 01227 462520 ⓦ www.clubchemistry. co.uk ⓛ Typically 21.00–02.00 on open nights

▶ *Take a trip to the seaside: Herne Bay is only a short journey away*

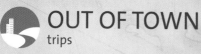
OUT OF TOWN
trips

Whitstable

Likeable Whitstable is famous for its oysters and an **annual oyster festival** in July, just one entry on the town's lively cultural calendar (ⓦ www.whitstableoysterfestival.com). Like many picturesque littoral spots, Whitstable has drawn in creative types over the years, and its arts community joins the succulent mollusc among the town's highlights. It's also a traditional seaside holiday resort, alive with quaint tea rooms, cheerful chippies and a peaceful, pretty shingle beach – one of the few in England to have a pub on it. ⓦ www.seewhitstable.com

GETTING THERE

The coastal resort is in the district of Canterbury, about 8 km (5 miles) north of the city. If you're not driving, Whitstable is well served by bus from Canterbury, with services including the 4, 5, 6, 7 (sometimes with a letter suffix) plus Unibus routes among the public transport options; allow about half an hour. The train journey requires a change and will take longer.

SIGHTS & ATTRACTIONS

Whitstable Castle

This smart 18th-century castle is not open on a regular schedule for tourists but public events are held here and group visits can be arranged. There are also some attractive gardens and the Orangery tea rooms. ⓐ Tower Hill ⓣ 01227 281726 ⓦ www.whitstablecastle.co.uk

Whitstable Harbour

Built in 1831 to help carry coals from Newcastle to Canterbury, the harbour's history has encompassed diving, shipbuilding, fishing and world trade. It remains a working port, though there are now also more tourist-friendly attractions such as recreation, retail and refreshments. ⓦ www.whitstableharbour village.co.uk

CULTURE

Whitstable Museum & Gallery

Matters maritime prevail here, with displays on oysters and shipping, plus seascapes alongside a look at the shoreline's resident wildlife. ⓐ 5a Oxford Street ⓣ 01227 276998 ⓦ www.canterbury.gov.uk ⓛ 10.00–16.00 Mon–Sat, closed Sun (Sept–June); 10.00–16.00 Mon–Sat, 13.00–16.00 Sun (July & Aug)

● *Colourful stands adorn the Whitstable waterfront*

RETAIL THERAPY

Fish Market Piscatorial purchases aplenty at this undercover market. Eat on site or take the raw ingredients home. ⓐ South Quay ⓣ 01227 771245 ⓛ 08.00–17.00 daily

TAKING A BREAK

Caffe Eighty Nine £–££ The close proximity of the tables is the only drawback at this popular place, though there is some outside seating. A comprehensive café menu includes breakfasts, bagels, paninis, pastries, cakes, scones and smoothies, all with a gratifying price to quality ratio. ⓐ 89 Tankerton Road ⓣ 07751 327587 ⓛ 09.00–17.30 Mon–Sat, 10.00–17.30 Sun, 10.00–17.00 bank holidays

Restaurant de la Côte ££–£££ This well-run restaurant serves up both traditional and contemporary continental cuisine. Local ingredients are crafted into entrées such as slow-cooked shoulder of Romney Marsh lamb and Coq au Vin, as well as exclusive eats like partridge. ⓐ 101 Tankerton Road ⓣ 01227 281180 ⓦ www.la-cote.co.uk ⓛ 12.00–14.30 lunch, 14.30–17.00 afternoon tea, 18.30–21.30 dinner Tues–Sat, 12.00–14.30 Sun, closed Mon

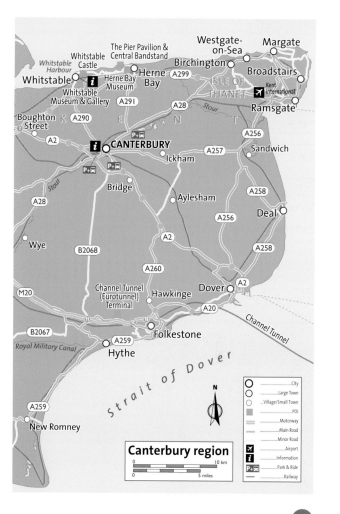

Canterbury region

○	City
○	Large Town
○	Village/Small Town
■	POI
	Motorway
	Main Road
	Minor Road
✈	Airport
i	Information
P+🚍	Park & Ride
	Railway

Herne Bay

Traditional seaside frolics are the name of the game at Herne Bay, where candy-floss outlets and fish 'n' chip shops ply their trade against a background of Victorian architecture. Like most British seaside towns, it's a seasonal resort, with activity tailing off once the warm weather is over, so if you want to see the town at its best, go in summer. The **Herne Bay Cultural Trail** can help you seek out some of the town's attractions. The route map and further details about the 18 points of interest can be found on the website. Ⓦ www.hernebayculturaltrail.co.uk

GETTING THERE

Herne Bay is slightly further from Canterbury than Whitstable, 11 km (7 miles) north of the city. Buses 4, 5, 6, 7 (sometimes

● Herne Bay's picturesque waterfront

there's a letter afterwards) are among the more frequent services. Some school-oriented routes (with three-digit numbers beginning with 9) may also be of use. The journey time is about 45 minutes. Rail travel from Canterbury is not direct and the journey takes longer than the bus.

SIGHTS & ATTRACTIONS

Seafront

Herne Bay's chief lures lie on its shoreline. As well as the pleasant shingle beach and some well-tended sea gardens, there's the 1924 Central Bandstand, repository of a café and pub, and the iconic clock tower, said to hold the distinction of being the world's first freestanding purpose-built construction of the kind, which dates from 1837. The Pier Pavilion promises roller-skating, a sports hall, fitness and dance studios and squash. Other seaside fun ranges from mini golf to watersports.

Slightly back from the shore, the Western Esplanade and Central Parade (which form the coast road) have all the bingo and amusement arcades, chippies and cafés that the holidaymaker could desire. There are also some high-quality restaurants.

CULTURE

Herne Bay Museum

Old-fashioned holiday fun is celebrated at this modern museum, which also includes information about the town's clock tower (formerly the country's tallest), some archaeological finds, a World War II display and temporary art exhibitions.

ⓐ 12 William Street ☎ 01227 367368 ⏱ 10.00–16.00 Mon–Sat, last entry 15.45, closed Sun (Sept–June); 10.00–16.00 Mon–Sat, last entry 15.45, 13.00–16.00 Sun (July & Aug) ⓦ www.hernebay-museum.co.uk

RETAIL THERAPY

Bay Art Gallery Local and visiting artists display and sell their wares. ⓐ 47a Williams Street ☎ 01227 369876 ⓦ www.bayartgallery.co.uk ⏱ 10.00–16.00 on open days; see website for details

TAKING A BREAK

Gabriel's Restaurant ££ Fish with an Italian flavour is Gabriel's speciality, with the pasta dishes getting the gourmets gushing. ⓐ 122 Central Parade ☎ 01227 370360 ⏱ 12.00–22.00 ❶ Cash only

Le Petit Poisson £££ With an excellent location about as close to the sea as it is possible to get without being surrounded by the tide, this cosy, split-level restaurant serves mouthwatering entrées, such as shellfish, moules à la crème and moules marinières, in elegantly understated surroundings. ⓐ Pier Approach, Central Parade ☎ 01227 361199 ⓦ www.lepetitpoisson.co.uk ⏱ 12.00–14.30, 18.30–21.00 Tues–Fri, 12.00–14.30, 18.30–21.30 Sat, 12.00–15.30 Sun, closed Mon, except bank holidays

▶ *The King's Mile is full of architectural gems*

PRACTICAL
information

Directory

GETTING THERE

Flying

Canterbury is served by Kent International Airport, which receives daily Flybe (Ⓦ www.flybe.com) flights from Edinburgh and frequent flights from Manchester. Other minor domestic destinations and a handful of European cities also have direct services. London's two main airports, Heathrow and Gatwick, are no more than a couple of hours away.

Many people are aware that air travel emits CO_2, which contributes to climate change. You may be interested in the possibility of lessening the environmental impact of your flight through the charity **Climate Care** (Ⓦ www.jpmorganclimate care.com), which offsets your CO_2 by funding environmental projects around the world.

Driving

From central London, it's about a 100-km (60-mile) drive along the A2 and M2 to Canterbury, which should take you about an hour and 40 minutes if traffic is light. From the north of England, you will circumnavigate London on the M25. The route-planner function on the AA website can give you precise directions and a time estimate. Ⓦ www.theaa.com

Rail travel

The train is the most time-efficient option, with direct services from London St Pancras to Canterbury West the fastest, taking just under an hour. Several London terminuses serve the Kentish city, either directly or with one change. Standard fares seem to be in the region of £23–30, regardless of how far in advance you book. From further north than London, you will have to change in the capital.

National Rail Enquiries ⓦ www.nationalrail.co.uk
The Trainline ⓦ www.thetrainline.com

Coach

The most economical means of travelling from London to Canterbury is by coach, which can often cost under £10 even at quite short notice. Frequent services depart each day, taking between an hour and a half and two hours. If you're coming from further north, the lengthy journey time could be a deterrent to coach travel – seven hours minimum from Manchester, for example.

National Express ⓦ www.nationalexpress.com

HEALTH, SAFETY AND CRIME

Canterbury is not a dangerous city, but it's wise to follow the usual advice when visiting a new place: avoid being alone in deserted areas, especially after dark, keep valuables concealed and give a wide berth to drunken groups – not that these are a common sight around town. Should you visit Herne Bay or Whitstable and take to the English Channel, exercise the appropriate precautions as regards water safety.

Emergency contacts

Canterbury Police Station ⓐ Old Dover Road ⓣ 999 or 112 for emergencies; 01622 690690 for non-emergencies

ⓦ www.kent.police.uk ⓒ 08.00–20.00 Mon–Sat, 10.00–18.00
Sun & bank holidays

The nearest accident and emergency (A&E) department to
Canterbury is in Ashford at the William Harvey Hospital
ⓐ Kennington Road, Willesborough ⓣ 01233 633331
ⓦ www.nhs.uk

For non-urgent medical help, the NHS Direct line is 0845
4647, or you can go online at ⓦ www.nhsdirect.nhs.uk

OPENING HOURS

Canterbury's places of interest usually open from around 10.00
to 17.00 – though large places may open an hour earlier and
close later, while the opposite is often the case for small sites.
Places of interest may be shut on Monday and sometimes
Sunday. Opening hours are often reduced on Sunday and in the
winter, especially at largely outdoor attractions. Banks and
offices are typically open from 09.00 to 17.00 on weekdays;
banks might also work a half-day on Saturday. Shops tend to
trade from 09.00 or 09.30 to 17.00 or 18.00 for six days. Trading
law permits only six hours of business for retailers on Sunday,
but there's usually a local corner shop selling essentials outside
standard hours.

TOILETS

Tourist attractions, restaurants, pubs and hotels will always have
WCs. Blocks of public toilets are scattered throughout the city,
though they may be open only for 'office' hours. If caught short
around the cathedral area, the first floor of Debenhams has
a restroom.

CHILDREN

There are plenty of activities for children to enjoy in Canterbury.
The Canterbury Tales (see pages 61–2) is a great choice, while
exhibits at the **Museum of Canterbury** and **Roman Museum** (see
pages 62–4 and 49–50), though less uproarious, have also been
devised with young visitors in mind. A **punt** on the river is sure
to delight children (see page 20); the haunted river tour could be
entertaining (see page 20), and along the same lines there's the
Canterbury Ghost Tour (ⓦ www.canterburyghosttour.com).
Outdoor fun can be had at one of the city's green spaces or the
out-of-town seaside resorts of **Herne Bay** (see pages 86–8) and
Whitstable (see pages 82–4).

TRAVELLERS WITH DISABILITIES

The **Disabled Go** (ⓦ www.disabledgo.com) site contains listings
of venues in Canterbury (over a thousand in the district) that
have been assessed on accessibility criteria. Many of the top
attractions have made adaptations to ensure inclusiveness.
Most local car parks have dedicated bays for disabled badge
holders and there are a couple of facilities entirely for their use.
The low buses of the Park and Ride scheme (see page 36) can
accommodate wheelchairs.

FURTHER INFORMATION
Canterbury Visitor Centre

As well as providing information about local attractions, the
visitor centre can help with accommodation.

ⓐ 12–13 Sun Street ⓣ 01227 378100 ⓦ www.canterbury.co.uk
ⓛ 09.00–17.30 Mon–Sat, 10.00–17.00 Sun

ACKNOWLEDGEMENTS

The photographs in this book were taken by Grant Rooney for Thomas Cook Publishing, to whom the copyright belongs, except for the following: Trustees of Eastbridge Hospital, page 57.

Project editor: Jennifer Jahn
Copy editor: Cath Senker
Layout: Trevor Double
Proofreaders: Rosemary Moore & Rachel Norridge
Indexer: Marie Lorimer

AUTHOR BIOGRAPHY

Debbie Stowe is a freelance journalist, travel writer and author. She has written around 20 non-fiction and travel books, specialising in UK, Indian Ocean and Eastern European destinations. Her writing also covers the natural world, film, human rights, cultural and social issues.

Send your thoughts to
books@thomascook.com

- **Found a great bar, club, shop or must-see sight that we don't feature?**
- **Like to tip us off about any information that needs a little updating?**
- **Want to tell us what you love about this handy little guidebook and more importantly how we can make it even handier?**

Then here's your chance to tell all! Send us ideas, discoveries and recommendations today and then look out for your valuable input in the next edition of this title.

Email the above address (stating the title) or write to:
pocket guides Series Editor, Thomas Cook Publishing, PO Box 227, Coningsby Road, Peterborough PE3 8SB, UK.